YOUR FRESH START

ALEXANDRA GRACE SCOTT
a fellow traveler on the road of life

The words I have written here are from my heart to yours. You have survived some of life's most difficult challenges, and it's my desire to help you. Your personal challenges may have left you defeated, discouraged and in despair. I want you to know that *I care*.

WHO AM I AND WHY AM I SHARING THIS?

Years ago I found myself with two children, divorced, experiencing post-traumatic stress disorder, with little money, a health challenge and a bleak future. I knew that to move forward I had to rally myself.

I needed to make some changes. I call these changes the Seven Healing Choices.

My aim is to help you find the power of CHOICE that exists within you. These Seven Healing Choices have been "tested" and proven to work - by me and many others faced with homelessness and severe hardships.

These Seven Healing Choices will help you to experience peace and a better life. These are gentle shifts you can make through your ability to choose.

When I made these choices, they brought a much needed healing and a new way of thinking and feeling *(yes, you can shift feelings!)*. I searched for answers to help me find some strength, have a plan and just a spark of confidence and hope.

What I found are these Seven Healing Choices. Making these choices, I was able to go forward from just "surviving" day to day.

Positive things happened in my life, doors opened and I was able to be my "better self" – in my relationships, my job, and with my family. I became financially independent.

For a number of years I've shared these Healing Choices with the women at Burckle Place, a transitional housing program for single homeless women founded by the Lord's Place. I have seen the positive results first hand.

If you can make shifts in your thinking, the result will be changes in what you do - and what actually shows up in your life. Making healing choices is up to us - it's an "inside job" and a choice only we can make.

YOUR FRESH START can happen today!

Alexandra Grace

ALEXANDRA GRACE SCOTT

TAKE THE FIRST STEP IN FAITH. YOU DON'T HAVE TO SEE THE WHOLE STAIRCASE. JUST TAKE THE FIRST STEP.

MARTIN LUTHER KING, JR

*Rising out of homelessness, helplessness
and hopelessness can begin today. Before
the outer can change, the inner needs to
be looked at and put in order.
That part is up to us!*

HEALING CHOICE ONE

To move forward
FORGIVE YOURSELF

In order to move forward we need mental,
emotional and physical strength. That's
why it is critical to start by forgiving yourself. We can then release these "mistakes"
and allow ourselves to move forward.

Holding onto regrets, shame and blame
weakens our inner strength. We can become
paralyzed when we're drowning in guilt,
self-hate and anger.

Healing through choosing self-forgiveness
is a vital first step that helps us to:
• make better choices
• build healthier self-esteem
• have greater self-appreciation
• have a brighter future

As Lucille Ball once said,
"Love yourself
first and everything else
falls into line. You really
have to love yourself to
get anything done in
this world."

Negative emotions do nothing good for us,
and just drag us down. We need to have
compassion for ourselves as human beings
surviving in this challenging world.

The past has passed.

Did you learn lessons from your experiences?

Self-forgiveness will allow you to release
shame and blame. This is key to moving
on to your new life and building a healthy
opinion of yourself.

*Take the lessons of your past
with you and move on.*

HEALING CHOICE TWO

To move on with your life
FORGIVE THE UNFORGIVABLE

Forgiveness of others is crucial because it heals us. Try viewing those who have hurt you as having mental and emotional issues. Forgiveness does not excuse the wrong.

Our past frustrations, anger and rage are certainly understandable and valid. However, maintaining the outrage over life's hurts and injustices creates negative emotions that are harmful. These emotions release stress chemicals that affect the body, the mind, and weaken us.

Resentment keeps us stuck in the same place (the past), preventing us from moving forward with positive emotions.

Here's a prayer to help you remove past hurts and clear the way for healing. It certainly may be tough to say, but saying this will start healing the hurt, the anger, and make you stronger. *It's worth it.*

Think of the person(s) who have hurt you, and pray:
"I'm sorry this happened. I forgive you. May God bless you. Thank you."

Do this for yourself, for your own healing.

This prayer will clear the path for good to come forth into your life.

"When I started counting my blessings, my whole life turned around."
WILLIE NELSON

HEALING CHOICE **THREE**

The power of gratitude
BE GRATEFUL

Being truly grateful daily is one of the most powerful practices. It affects your body, mind, relationships and energy *all day long*. When we face difficulties in life, it can be hard to be grateful for anything. Feeling appreciation every day for the smallest things increases our happiness level. Gratitude also releases toxic feelings like resentment, frustration, regret and depression. It increases both mental and physical strength.

Gratitude helps in healing trauma. Exchange self-pity for gratitude. This practice will change your day, your chemistry and your life.

Gratitude:
- reduces toxic emotions
- increases happiness
- reduces depression and stress
- improves physical health

What are you grateful for today?

Think of three things you are grateful for right now. Write them down, if you can. Research has proven that if you do this for just 21 days, you will be a happier, more positive person. *It works!*

Gratitude is a healing choice you can make daily.

HEALING CHOICE FOUR

Your mind is yours to control
CHOOSING YOUR THOUGHTS
& FEELINGS

We have the ability to influence our attitude and moods everyday by choosing our thoughts and feelings. The alternative is to believe we have no control over our thoughts and let life and our thoughts just happen to us.

"Automatic" thinking is mainly negative. *(Studies have shown that as much as 75% of thinking is negative.)*

The good news is we have an inner capability given to us by the Creator - the power of choice. This remarkable ability gives us inner control when we feel life is out of control. We need to watch our thoughts. We have the ability to choose and create positive thoughts that provide us with power.

Positive thoughts = Positive results.

HEALING CHOICE FIVE

Find direction and your strength
DISCOVER SILENCE

We live in a world of constant noise and distraction, and can hardly "hear ourselves think." Being in silence has a power all of its own.

Silence allows messages to flow to us. It has been my experience that silence helps me find who I am. It brings me solutions, guidance and direction.

Silence for even a minute reduces stress, brings calmness, and provides clearer thinking. Silence allows you to discover your true self.

I discovered a simple, powerful technique to experience the silence within. It's Heart Focused Breathing. Take a minute and try this for yourself.

Breathe a little more deeply than normal.

Breathe in 5-6 seconds and breathe out 5-6 seconds. Imagine you are breathing from your heart.

To help you focus on your heart you can place your hand over your heart.

Scientists have discovered the heart possesses a special intelligence *(a knowing and feeling)* that communicates to us.

Discover the silence within by practicing this daily, whatever is going on around you.

Listen to the desires of your heart as you practice being in silence. They will point the way to who you are and what you need to do.

Being in silence reveals your truth.

HEALING CHOICE SIX

Believe in yourself
CREATE SELF-CONFIDENCE

When I was at my lowest, to move forward I had to believe in myself. Moving on from a place of desperation, I had to find things to appreciate about myself.

Here's what I realized -
I am a creation with unique DNA and abilities – an intelligent design created by an Intelligent Creator.

You are one of a kind.

Believe in your unique self, with a unique personality and abilities. Like each snowflake and each flower, you are truly unique.

Another powerful tool to create self-confidence is to close your eyes and imagine a movie screen in your mind. See and feel yourself in the movie of your new life.

This kind of visualization is very powerful. Athletes use it to enhance their performance with astonishing results. Muhammed Ali used mental and verbal practices to impact his performance. He shared perhaps the simplest yet most powerful statement of self-worth, *"I am the greatest!"*

Use visualization to find, see and become your best self.

Low self-confidence brings a feeling of weakness, low motivation and sadness. Instead, choose to feel like a child of God made of divine substance *(we possess the same properties as stardust!)*.

Stand tall, smile! You know more than you think you know. You are stronger than you think you are. Talk to yourself like you would to someone you love. Tune into what you like about yourself and your abilities.

Self love and appreciation of what is right about ourselves is essential to going forward *Rejection of ourselves is self abuse.*

Our failures are events, *not* who we are!

HEALING CHOICE **SEVEN**

Believe in your future
FIND YOUR POTENTIAL,
PURPOSE & PLAN

We need a plan to build anything and make it a reality. It can be as simple as writing down your goals and action steps.

Decide what you want.

You can start small by thinking of what you want for the rest of this week, the month, and the year.

Life is a process. You have the power to not give up! You can't accomplish what you want if you give up the belief that you can and will do something.

Without action, you aren't going anywhere. If you make a plan, you will be more motivated to take action. Your future is built through the actions of the present. So take small steps forward. It's more about going

forward and taking some action toward
your intended destination.

Inaction makes us feel doubt and fear,
which could lead us to giving up. Taking
action makes us feel hopeful and more
confident. It increases our courage and
self-worth.

Identify what is holding you back
What can you do to make it better?
If you experience a setback, believe
it's part of the process and a detour
leading you to another door.

99% of failures occur because someone
believed that a setback was a defeat.
Look for the positive in everything.
It's never too late to begin.

You can do it!

Find support for your vision and your
goals through a program, counselor,
spiritual leader or an individual who
believes in you!

Believe in yourself.

THE SEVEN HEALING CHOICES

The Seven Healing Choices outlined in this booklet can change your attitude, energy and outlook to one that is more positive.

The Seven Healing Choices will make a difference in your life.

Remember that small shifts in our thinking create big shifts in our lives.

Going forward make your life count by making a difference in the lives of others – a kind act, a smile, a word of encouragement.

Share your story of letting go of the past and how you gave yourself a "fresh start."

Volunteer to help others. You will build self-confidence and self-esteem.

Service to others helps you to know you are making a difference in this world.

Making the choice to incorporate the Seven Healing Choices in your life reflects your willingness to take the next step in -

- Belief *(that you can overcome difficulties)*
- Action *(knowing that no change comes without action)*

I have shared the Seven Healing Choices with love and with the sincere hope that you use them to make YOUR FRESH START.

Alexandra Grace

ALEXANDRA GRACE SCOTT

www.ingramcontent.com/pod-product-compliance
Lightning Source LLC
Chambersburg PA
CBHW051255020426
42333CB00025B/3214